CHEROKEE NATION

Keowee

NORTH CAROLINA

Wm. Bartram's uncle's plantation

SOUTH CAROLINA

Fort Moore

Augusta

ATLANTIC OCEAN

GEORGIA

found seed of Franklinia tree

Charleston

Savannah

Alatamaha River

CREEK NATION

Cumberland Island

FLORIDA

ship wrecked

St. Augustine

Talahasochte

St. Johns River

SEMINOLE NATION

Mosquito Lagoon

A Map
of the
Travels of

William
Bartram

1773–1776

For Frances Foster

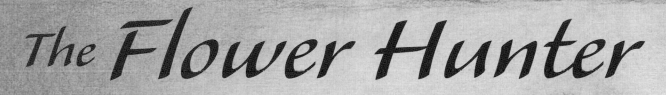

The Flower Hunter

William Bartram, America's First Naturalist

Deborah Kogan Ray

Frances Foster Books

Farrar, Straus and Giroux

New York

Journal of Wm. Bartram:

begun on my eighth birthday,
20 April 1747
Bartram Farm, Kingsessing,
His Majesty's colony
of Pennsylvania

My father, John Bartram, is a botanist.
He studies plants and trees. I help him
with his work. My name is William, but
everyone calls me Billy. Father calls me
his "little botanist."

September 1747

Father and I collected seeds from the red maple trees today

Long before I was born, Father planted a few red maple trees from seeds he had collected. More trees planted themselves when the wind carried their seeds all over our hillside. Father says we are doing the work of the wind when we gather seeds to plant in other places.

Red Maple
(Acer rubrum)

We will pack our collection into big wooden boxes, which contain many kinds of seeds that Father has found in his travels. They will be shipped across the ocean to England, where there is much curiosity about American plants.

After dinner, I started a drawing of a red maple leaf. With the leaf as a model, I sketched the outline and stem as exactly as I could because a botanical drawing must be accurate. When I showed my picture to Father, he said, "Very fine rendering, Billy."

He lent me his magnifying glass so that I could see the intricate patterns of the leaf's veins. They formed designs that looked like Father's maps of faraway rivers and mountains. Father has explored for plants in places few Americans have been. He has met French fur traders and sat with the chiefs of the Six Indian Nations at Onondaga.

I dream of the day when he will take me with him.

April 1748
On my ninth birthday

When spring comes, I have little time for drawing. There are many farm chores, and everyone in the family must help. Father was a farmer long before he studied the science of botany. His experiments to improve crops led to his wanting to learn how plants grow.

Father and my older brothers plow and plant the fields for the wheat, oat, flax, and corn that we grow for market. Mother and my sisters plant the large kitchen garden that provides vegetables for our family of eleven. There are nine children—four are older than me, three are younger, and I have a twin sister.

I tilled two acres for flowers that are grown for seed we sell, and I planted herbs in Father's medicinal garden. Every day, I help him tend the bushes and trees in his experimental nursery. That is where he cultivates the many varieties of plants found on his wilderness travels.

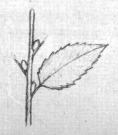

Budding

Father is teaching me to identify plant families by examining the shape of the leaves, the structure of the seeds, buds, and flowers, the bark and branching patterns of trees. Some are difficult to identify because they resemble other plants. But I have begun to recognize many, and Father says I am learning quickly.

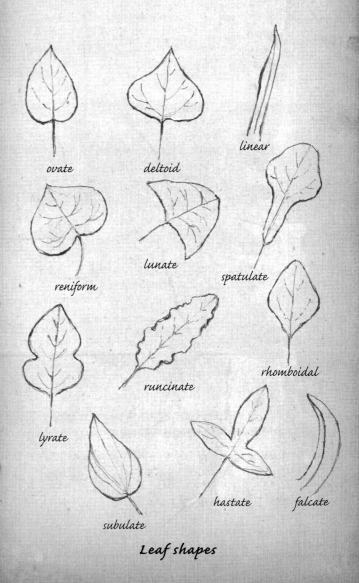

ovate *deltoid* *linear*

reniform *lunate* *spatulate*

lyrate *runcinate* *rhomboidal*

subulate *hastate* *falcate*

Leaf shapes

Mr. Franklin explained electricity to me today

Father's best friend, Benjamin Franklin, came to visit. He arrived as thunder crashed and a rainstorm began. "Come, Billy," he called, "let us watch nature's display."

It took all my courage to go outside with him, for I have always feared thunderstorms. As we watched lightning bolts crackle and light up the sky, Mr. Franklin explained that he is studying nature's great electrical power, to learn how to harness this energy for scientific purposes.

Like Father, Mr. Franklin is interested in all the ways of nature. They spent the afternoon talking about the formation of mountains, the flow of oceans, and the composition of stars.

I was not supposed to be listening, but I want to learn about the ways of nature, too. Mother caught me in my hiding place behind the stairs and told me not to eavesdrop.

April 1750

A short journey with Father

Today, Father and I ferried across the Delaware River to Cedar Creek in New Jersey. The fiddlehead ferns, trillium, and other woodland flowers were emerging. The mosses were greening. It was a perfect time to be collecting them.

As we searched the forest floor, I spied pink lungwort—a species of *Pulmonaria*. I recognized it from a description in Father's botanical notes. He congratulated me on my discovery. He has found this variety only once, he said.

I have lately become interested in studying and drawing birds and other wildlife, as well as plants. I sketched a blue heron before we departed Cedar Creek.

My journeys with Father end too quickly. I have accompanied him overnight but have never been allowed too far from home. He says I am not yet old enough. But he admits that he often gets lonely on his long journeys. I hope that very soon Father will let me be his wilderness companion.

September 1753

My first long journey with Father to the Catskill Mountains in New York

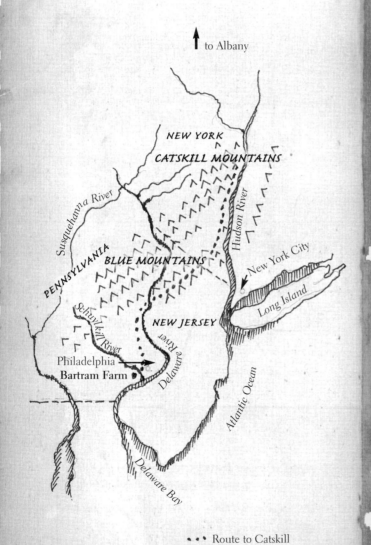

to Albany

NEW YORK

CATSKILL MOUNTAINS

Susquehanna River

Hudson River

BLUE MOUNTAINS

New York City

PENNSYLVANIA

Long Island

Schuylkill River

NEW JERSEY

Delaware River

Philadelphia

Bartram Farm

Atlantic Ocean

Delaware Bay

• • • Route to Catskill Mountains

At last, I am bound for the wilderness. Father and I saddled our horses and departed Kingsessing for the Catskill Mountains on the first day of this month.

We rode ninety miles due north, crossed the Blue Mountains of New Jersey, then traveled another hundred miles through the Hudson River highlands in New York. On the fifth day, we left our horses at the inn where we had spent the night and began a long and steep hike to the Great Falls of Catskill. We carried no water, as Father had found many cool springs along this route on his previous visit. But all of them had dried up in this summer's drought. Finally, we reached a small clear lake, where we quenched our thirst and rested.

I heard the thunder of the Great Falls long before I saw them. When I scrambled up a high rock ledge, I beheld a roaring cascade that plummeted into a deep chasm. Water spray filled the air. Never could I have imagined such a sight.

Catskill Mountains

For days we have been exploring these wondrous mountains on horseback and on foot.

I climbed granite peaks that cradle the clouds. Father and I gathered mayapple in the shadow of towering forests; wild cherries are plentiful in the valleys. Our saddlebags are bulging with spruce seedlings that we dug and wrapped in burlap.

At night, we camp under the stars on beds of feathered moss.

Today, I scaled tall firs to collect their cones. Father and I climbed a crumbling cliff and found fossils of fish engraved in stone.

In the glow of the setting sun, I watched eagles soar and sketched a gloriously colored rattlesnake.

My skill at drawing wildlife and plants improves. I told Father that I wish to spend my life portraying nature's beauty. He said he thinks it a noble ambition, but he fears drawing pictures will never afford me a reasonable living.

But I care nothing about riches, except those that exist in nature.

April 1755

*Kingsessing, His Majesty's colony
of Pennsylvania
On my sixteenth birthday*

We are living in a general state of alarm.
Entire families are being murdered and
scalped, their farms burned to the ground.

France and Britain have been arguing
about who should possess territory in
America. The French have encouraged
uprisings among the native people, and the
British have placed huge rewards on the
heads of the tribal chiefs. Many colonists
have armed themselves and gone in pursuit
of the reward.

Mr. Franklin has established a home
guard to protect Philadelphia and nearby
towns. We disagree with our old friend on the
matter of bearing arms. As Quakers, we will
not participate in the taking of human life.
Father holds that the needless killing of any
creature of this earth is wrong, and I agree.

But our family remains concerned about
the possibility of attack. Mother has equipped
a hiding place for us in the root cellar.

Throughout the winter, I checked for
footprints in the snowy woods above the river.
We are wary whenever we see a stranger at
the boundary of our farm.

Father has canceled our
botanical expedition to the mountains of
Virginia that was scheduled for this month.

It is now too dangerous to travel in
wilderness areas.

July 1765

Cape Fear, North Carolina–
Father has been appointed
"His Majesty's Botanist for North
America" by King George III

After seven years of bloody conflict, the French and Indian War ended two years ago. The Treaty of Paris gave Britain all the territory east of the Mississippi River. Father's duty as His Majesty's Botanist for North America is to explore this new territory. He is to gather plant specimens, study the soil and weather conditions for planting crops, and map the rivers.

"Billy, does thee wish to accompany me?" Father wrote. His letter reached me at the trading post that I set up four years ago on the Cape Fear River. Though I have no talent for business, the store has provided a small income while I pursue my painting and study of plants and bird migrations.

Within a week, I sold my stock at auction, packed my art supplies, and happily prepared to set off to meet Father. My duty will be to draw pictures of the plants and wildlife that we encounter on our journey.

September 1765

Charleston, His Majesty's colony of South Carolina

Since Father's ship arrived in the city of Charleston, we have purchased horses, obtained what scanty maps we can find, and arranged with brokers for the care and transport of the plants that will be shipped to England. Father has written letters to traders who will provide us with canoes and guides for hire, and to dignitaries we hope to visit along our route.

Our plan is to go as far into the wilderness of East and West Florida as the Indian nations will permit.

Father's heart is young, but his body is not. He has declared that this will be his last long expedition.

October 1765

St. Augustine, His Majesty's territory of East Florida

For the past six weeks, Father and I have followed the coastal waterways from Charleston to this old Spanish settlement in East Florida.

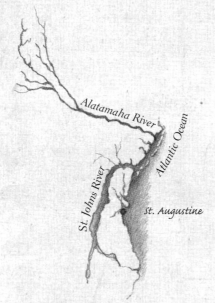

In the course of our journey, we lost our way along the winding Alatamaha River in Georgia.

As darkness fell, we found a spot for camping along the riverbank and resigned ourselves to wait for morning.

We awoke to a discovery. Beside our campsite grew a small tree that we had never seen in any of our travels. We examined the leaves, bark, and structure of its branches, but they did not reveal its family. Since the tree was not in bloom, we could not identify the species by the flower.

We explored the riverbank and found several more examples, but were unable to gain any other information. Nor did I have an opportunity to make but a hasty sketch of the tree, as Father was anxious to find a route back. He regretted that we found no seeds for further study and hoped that in the course of our travels we would come across this mysterious tree again.

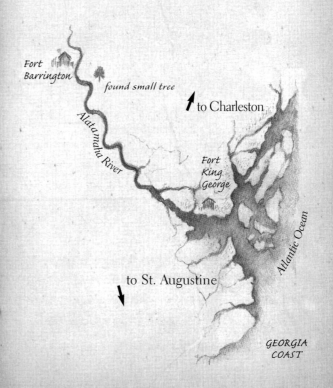

St. Augustine, His Majesty's territory of East Florida

We have returned to St. Augustine to prepare the maps and reports of our expedition. We were trying to reach the source of the St. Johns River, but were forced to turn back when the dense growth of reeds and plants prevented further passage upriver.

We experienced severe weather and many problems traveling in this southern climate. It has been so hot that the horses were near collapse. It has rained with such intensity that placid creeks swelled with raging currents.

Father nearly drowned when our canoe capsized. He saved himself by clinging to tree roots until I could right the canoe and paddle to his aid.

Despite the difficulties, I am much taken with the giant forests, wild dark swamplands, and green savannas.

My journey with Father is nearly ended. He will be returning to Philadelphia soon, but it is agreed that I will remain here in East Florida to continue exploring this land, which is unlike any I have known.

September 1776

Savannah, colony of Georgia
My explorations of North and
South Carolina, Georgia, and East
and West Florida are now completed

It is ten years since I said goodbye to my father in St. Augustine.

I have come to Savannah to send the last of my plant specimens and a crate of my paintings and drawings by ship to Pennsylvania, before I return overland. I was fortunate to find a vessel to take them. Trade routes are threatened because our colonies are at war with Britain.

In July, the bell was rung in Philadelphia to proclaim America's independence. The news has only now reached me.

My search for plants has taken me into wilderness that few Americans know exists. I have lived with the people of the Choctaw, Creek, and Cherokee nations. They taught me their customs and language, and guided me on their forest trails.

The Seminole people invited me to feast on watermelon and oranges at their harvest celebration. They called me Puc Puggy, which means "flower hunter."

En route to Philadelphia

Though it has been, for the most part, a
solitary journey, I have not been lonely.
The creatures that inhabit the mountains,
swamplands, and meandering rivers have
been my traveling companions.

Nature has been my teacher, and I have
followed its paths with an open heart to learn
its wonders.

I fell asleep to the night howl of wolves
and hooting owls and awakened to the
morning call of loons.

In a dark swamp, I was terror-struck as
alligators battled fiercely.

I traveled by canoe and sailboat, on
horseback and on foot. I gathered mountain
laurel and lichen on rocky peaks. In the
lagoons of tropical forests, I observed fish,
turtles, and water birds. I was snowbound in
the Appalachians and shipwrecked on a
sea-swept island off the coast of Florida in a
summer hurricane. Through the seasons,
I wrote my scientific notes and painted
hundreds of pictures.

My travels took me far into the west—a
journey of 2,400 miles. I stood on the banks of
the great Mississippi River on America's frontier.

January 1777

Bartram Farm, Kingsessing, colony of Pennsylvania

Today, I returned to our farm on the banks of the Schuylkill River.

My brothers and sisters and their children gathered. Nieces and nephews, born during my absence, were introduced to me. It is a shock to see the changes that time has brought. Mother's hair has turned white, and Father is nearly blind. I fear his days as a botanist are over.

Everyone was eager to hear of my adventures. Father paid close attention to each scientific detail. The story that pleased him most was of the small tree that we discovered together when we were lost on the Alatamaha River. Last summer, I returned to the same riverbank and found the tree in full and fragrant bloom. I described the flowers to Father as very large, of snow-white color, and ornamented with a crown of gold. It was a remarkable species, for it bore ripe fruit simultaneously.

Sadly, Father could not see the picture I had painted, but I think he formed a mental image from my description.

I gave him the handful of seeds that I had collected. Though I searched as far as the Mississippi River, I never found another tree of its kind.

We decided that so rare a tree must be given a special name. We named it in honor of our old friend Benjamin, and for its place of discovery—*Franklinia alatamaha*.

We will plant the seeds in the spring.

Franklinia alatamaha, hand-colored engraving by William Bartram

Afterword

John and William Bartram planted the seeds of the *Franklinia alatamaha* on their farm in the spring of 1777.

John Bartram died in September of the same year. A fall from a tree left Billy crippled. He never traveled again, and spent the rest of his life at the farm in Kingsessing, writing, painting, and pursuing his studies of nature. He carried on his father's work as a botanist, cultivating many of the plants that he had collected on his solitary journey.

The Bartrams are credited with identifying and introducing into cultivation more than two hundred American plants and saving many species that would otherwise have become extinct.

Today, no Franklin trees remain on the banks of the Altamaha River, but thousands grow in gardens across the world from Billy's handful of seeds.

John Bartram (1699–1777)

John Bartram was America's first great botanist and plant explorer. Lacking a formal education, he taught himself botany and other sciences through observation, reading, and correspondence with equally inquiring minds in the colonies and abroad. With his best friend, Benjamin Franklin, he founded the American Philosophical Society in 1743.

John Bartram built his own house and designed and planted all his gardens. George Washington and Thomas Jefferson, who shared an interest in botany, were among the many notable visitors who came to Kingsessing.

John Bartram traveled north to Lake Ontario, south to Florida, and west to the Ohio River in search of plants for his own garden, and specimens for Peter Collinson of the Royal Society of London and other collectors in England and Europe.

His scientific findings were published internationally and include "Journal of Trip to Kattskills with Billy," an account of the first long botanical excursion he made with his son.

William Bartram (1739–1823)

Billy Bartram became America's first naturalist. An artist, writer, botanist, and intrepid wilderness explorer, he devoted his life to the study of the natural environment.

He was America's first botanical artist. His renderings of flowers, birds, and wildlife are notable for their beauty as well as their scientific accuracy. He was called "the father of Pennsylvania ornithology" and is credited with naming 215 North American birds. He was also a pioneering ethnographer, whose sympathetic writings about the tribes of southeast America became a source of information about the social structures, ceremonies, and languages of the Cherokee, Choctaw, Creek, and Seminole nations.

His book *Travels*, published in 1791, chronicles his 2,400-mile solitary expedition through the wilderness of North and South Carolina, Georgia, and East and West Florida. It was the most extensive exploration of America made by any scientist at that time. *Travels* inspired Henry David Thoreau and Charles Darwin with its observations of the world of nature, Lewis and Clark carried it with them on their western expedition, and Samuel Taylor Coleridge drew on its lush imagery when writing his poem "Kubla Khan."

The Bartram Trail, which follows Billy's journey through the southern mountains, swamps, and savannas, has been preserved and is hiked by many people today.

Of his quest to find harmony with nature, William Bartram referred to himself as a "pilgrim." Contrary to the prevailing attitudes of the time, his was a lone voice urging protection of the land and respect for the native peoples.

He saw all people as equals and every living thing as part of a divinely created universe.

Bartram plants

Most of us refer to plants by their common names in whatever language we speak. Botanists identify plants by genus (a related group) and species (group members with common characteristics) by using Latin binomials (two-word names). Latin is the language understood by scientists all over the world.

The first word of a binomial describes the plant's genus; the second (species) explains the special characteristics of the genus member.

John and William Bartram first identified and described hundreds of America's plants. These are a few species, with their common and Latin botanical names.

Trees and shrubs

American Hazel (*Corylus americana*)
American Holly (*Ilex opaca*)
Balsam Fir (*Abies balsamea*)
Bayberry (*Myrica pensylvanica*)
Black Cherry (*Prunus serotina*)
Carolina Buckeye (*Aesculus sylvatica*)
Cranberry (*Vaccinium macrocarpon*)
Cucumber Tree (*Magnolia acuminata*)
Darlington Oak (*Quercus hemispherica*)
Flowering Dogwood (*Cornus florida*)
Highbush Cranberry (*Viburnum triloba*)
Mountain Laurel (*Kalmia latifolia*)
Papaw (*Asimina triloba*)
Paper Birch (*Betula papyrifera*)
St.-John's-Wort (*Hypericum kalmianum*)
Sweetspire (*Itea virginica*)
Wisteria (*Wisteria frutescens*)
Witch Hazel (*Hamamelis virginiana*)

Flowering vines and plants

Bee Balm (*Monarda didyma*)
Black-Eyed Susan (*Rudbeckia hirta*)
Devil's Walking-Stick (*Aralia spinosa*)
Fox Grape (*Vitis labrusca*)
Giant Sunflower (*Helianthus giganteus*)
Poison Ivy (*Rhus radicans*)
Rose Mallow (*Hibiscus pentacarpos*)
Trumpet Honeysuckle (*Lonicera sempervirens*)
Trumpet Vine (*Campsis radicans*)

Fever Tree
(*Pinckneya pubens*)

Oakleaf Hydrangea
(*Hydrangea quercifolia*)

Flame Azalea
(*Rhododendron calendulaceum*)

Ogeechee Lime
(*Nyssa ogeche*)

Large-Flowered Evening Primrose
(*Oenothera grandiflora*)

Purple Coneflower
(*Echinacea purpurea*)

Magnolia
(*Magnolia auriculata*)

Tarflower
(*Bejaria racemosa*)

Morning Glory
(*Ipomoea purpurea*)

Venus's-Flytrap
(*Dionaea muscipula*)

Author's Note

In this account, I have used some of the spellings and place-names common in William Bartram's time.

Kingsessing is the English spelling of the Native American word Chingsessing. It means "a place where there is a meadow."

The Blue Mountains is the old name for the section of the Appalachian ridge that crosses Pennsylvania and New Jersey.

I use the current spelling for the Catskill Mountains. The Dutch spelling, Kaaterskill or Kattskill, was used by John Bartram in the account of his trip with Billy.

Altamaha is the current spelling for the river in Georgia. The Bartrams believed the name to be spelled Alatamaha because that was the designation on the maps used for their explorations. *Franklinia alatamaha* remains the name for the Franklin tree.

My thanks to Historic Bartram's Garden and to the staff of the American Philosophical Society for answering my many questions, and for giving me the pleasure of spending hours holding William Bartram's original drawings in my hands.

Bibliography

Bartram, William. *Travels and Other Writings*. New York: Library of America, 1996.

Berkeley, Edmund, and Dorothy Smith. *The Life and Travels of John Bartram: Lake Ontario to the River St. John*. Gainesville, Fla.: University Presses of Florida, 1982.

Cruikshank, Helen G., ed. *John and William Bartram's America: Selections from the Writings of the Philadelphia Naturalists*. New York: Devin-Adair Publishers, 1990.

Fry, Joel T. "An International Catalog of North American Trees and Shrubs: The Bartram Broadside, 1783," *Journal of Garden History*, Vol. 16, Jan.–March, 1996.

Harper, Francis. *The Travels of William Bartram: Naturalist Edition*. Athens, Ga.: University of Georgia Press, 1998.

Van Doran, Mark, ed. *Travels of William Bartram*. New York: Dover, 1985.

Illustrations executed in transparent watercolor, gouache, and colored pencil on Arches 140 lb. hot-press watercolor paper

William Bartram's engraving of *Franklinia alatamaha*, courtesy of the American Philosophical Society

Copyright © 2004 by Deborah Kogan Ray
All rights reserved
Distributed in Canada by Douglas & McIntyre Ltd.
Printed in China by South China Printing Co. Ltd.
Designed by Barbara Grzeslo
First edition, 2003
10 9 8 7 6 5 4 3 2 1

Library of Congress Cataloging-in-Publication Data
Ray, Deborah Kogan.
    The flower hunter : William Bartram, America's first naturalist / Deborah Kogan Ray.
        p.   cm.
    Summary: Young Billy Bartram keeps a journal of his experiences learning about the plants of the colonial United States from his father, John Bartram, as they travel together gathering specimens and planting seeds.
    ISBN 0-374-34589-9
    1. Bartram, William, 1739–1823—Juvenile literature.
    2. Bartram, John, 1699–1777—Juvenile literature.
    3. Botanists—United States—Biography—Juvenile literature.   4. Naturalists—United States—Biography—Juvenile literature.   [1. Bartram, William, 1739–1823.
    2. Bartram, John, 1699–1777.   3. Botanists.   4. Naturalists.
    5. Scientists.]   I. Title.

QK26 .R38 2003
580'.92—dc21

                                            2002023186

Wavah Bald Peak
caught in blizzard

INDIAN NATIONS RESERVE

SPANISH TERRITORY

CHICKASAW NATION

APPALACHIAN MOUNTAINS

Mississippi River

CHOCTAW NATION

route to the Mississippi River

Coweta

Pointe Coupee

Mobile

WEST FLORIDA

Tensaw River

Pensacola

EAST

Mobile Bay

GULF of MEXICO

◇ Native Villages
● British Settlements